CHESTER'S EASIEST PIANO COURSE

Book 2

Written by Carol Barratt   Illustrated by Sarah Lenton

Chester Music

(A division of Music Sales Ltd.)
8/9 Frith Street, London W1D 3JB
Exclusive distributors: Music Sales Ltd., Newmarket Rd. Bury St. Edmunds, Suffolk, IP33 3YB

This book belongs to ....

Teachers and Parents

This comprehensive Piano Course, in three books, can be used by the youngest beginner. Various games and puzzles are included to help the pupil absorb the information by having fun at the same time.

To reinforce certain topics, suggestions for supplementary material — drawn from Chester Piano Teaching Material — have been added in italics at the bottom of certain pages. For Book 2 of this course, supplementary material has been drawn from the following books:

Chester's Music Puzzles Sets One & Two (CH 55831 & 55832)
Chester's Piano Starters Volumes One & Two (CH 55661 & 55662)
Warm Up with Chester Part One (CH 55768)

The range of notes is limited in the early stages so that the pupil can feel confident and not overpowered by so many written notes. Move on fairly quickly as the pieces should be well within the pupil's capabilities.   Enjoy yourselves!

Carol Barratt

ready to go

Hello — it's me again, Chester Junior.
Learning to play the Piano is fun, isn't it ?

Let's get started on Book Two — I can't wait!

Watch out for the rest of the gang — Mo, Bradley, Lizzie and Eric.

(My famous Dad, Chester, appears in the supplementary books.)

and me !

CHESTER'S CHART
HINTS AND REMINDERS

1. Listen as you play.

2. Hold your fingers in a curved shape and play on the tips of your fingers — as if you were holding a very small orange in each hand. Your hand is a bridge which mustn't collapse.

3. Your wrists should be level with your arms.

4. If your feet don't touch the floor, use a pile of thick books to put under your feet. Telephone Directories are good for this!

5. **Don't** look down at your hands.

6. Looking at the **shape** of the music before you play will help you become a good sight-reader (Steps, Skips and Jumps).

7. **Always** practise with the correct fingering.

8. If the piece uses hands playing together, practise hands separately and when each part is perfect, try it hands together **slowly**. You can always play the pieces faster when you really know them.

Can you name these notes?

Can you name these notes?

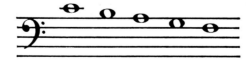

How many counts in each of these?

CURTAIN RAISER

C.B.

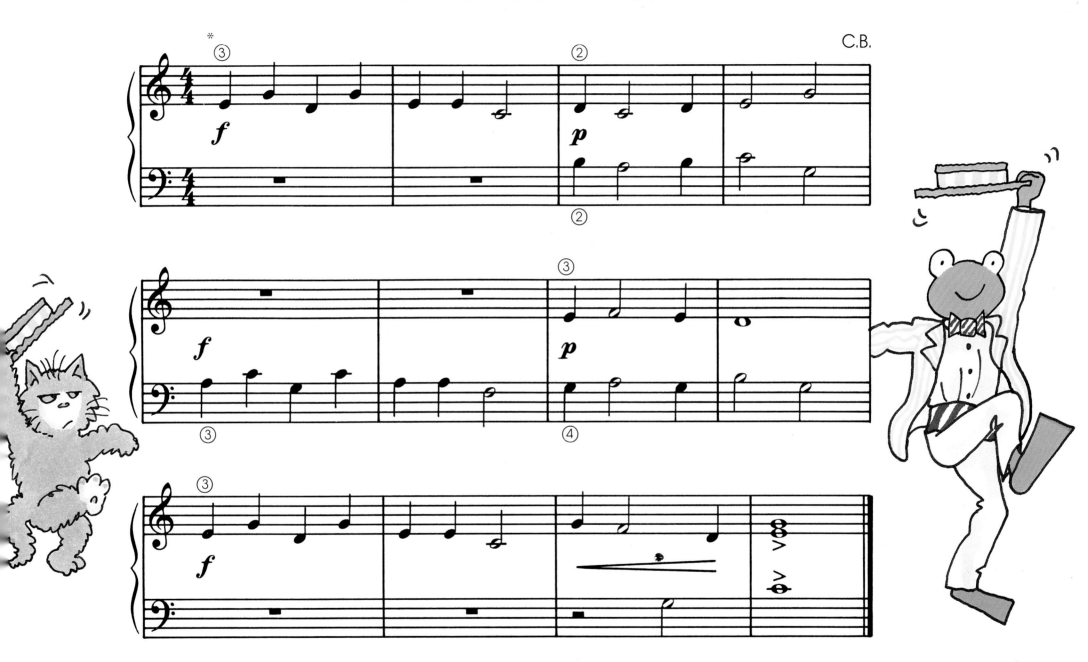

*In this book the finger numbers are in circles.

B FLAT
FLATS GO TO THE LEFT

♭ This is a Flat sign.

B FLAT is the black key just below **B**.

B♭

B

The pieces in *this* book use B♭ in the Left Hand only.

Each ♭ sign lasts a Bar.

B♭   B♭

FLAT ♭

that's easy to remember...

Think of Flatten Down!

Play all the **B♭**s on the Piano. Use either hand, any finger.

Find all the **E♭**s and **A♭**s on the Piano.

Try playing **B♭** and **A♭** together as a Chord with fingers ② and ③ of your ✋

Warm-up

Always move your hand **towards** the black key.

① ②

SCARBOROUGH FAIR

English Folk Song

Supplementary material: Chester's Piano Starters Volume One, p13.

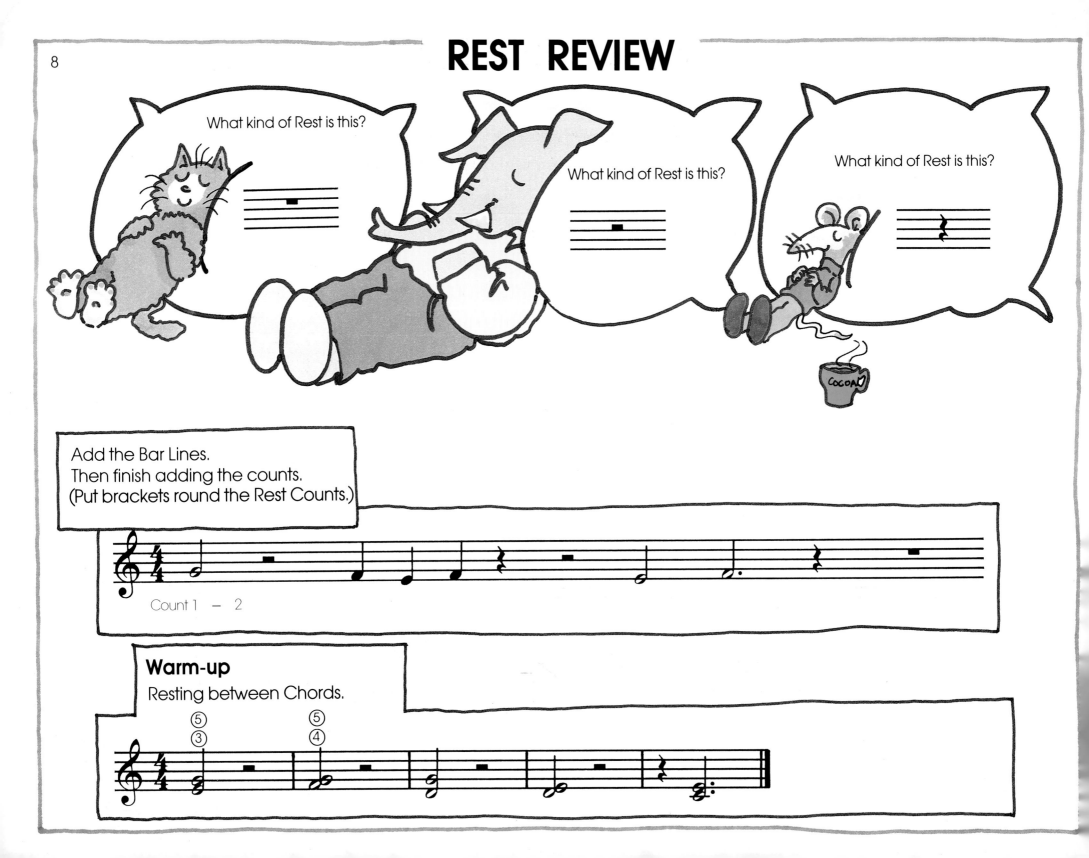

TAKE YOUR TIME

Look out for the Rests and the Tied notes.

Before playing this piece, tap out the rhythms on your knees using your left
knee for the Left Hand rhythm and your right knee for the Right Hand
rhythm.

Then try it knees together!

STEPS, SKIPS AND JUMPS

We learnt about these in Book One.

To remind you:
- A **STEP** is when a note steps up or down a note.
- A **SKIP** is when a note skips to the next-but-one note up or down.
- A **JUMP** is when a note jumps further than a Skip.

These are
also called

Some **STEPS**  **2nds**

Some **SKIPS**  **3rds**

Some **JUMPS**  **4ths**

 **5ths**

this is probably a 100th!

Play **C** with finger ① of your
Now make a Chord by adding the 3rd above.

Write this Chord here →

have a pencil ready...

Play **C** with finger ① of your
Now make a Chord by adding the 4th below.

Write this Chord here →

MOVING ALONG

Accompaniment

When you can play this piece,
try singing the tune by itself to see if you
can manage the Steps, Skips and Jumps.

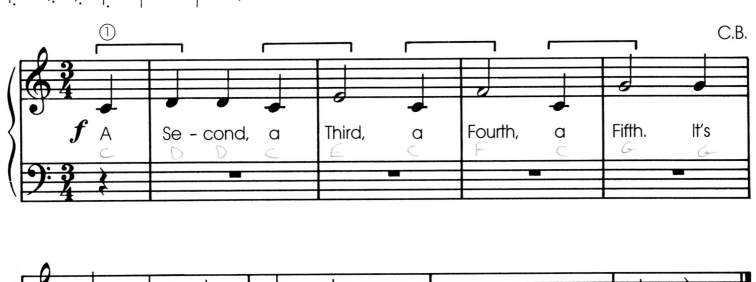

C.B.

f A Se - cond, a Third, a Fourth, a Fifth. It's
C D D C E C F C G G

ea - sy to fol - low the notes as they shift.
G F E F E G C C D E
G G A B C

I love 5ths

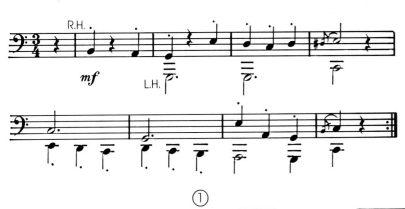

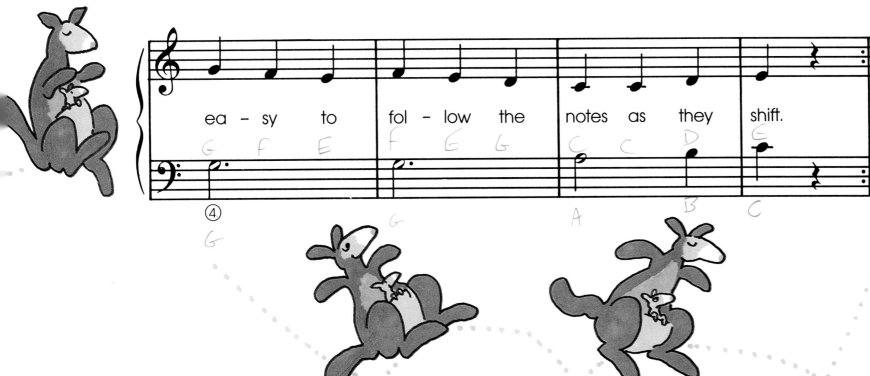

VOLUME CONTROL

$$p < f > p$$

The louds and softs in music are called **DYNAMICS**.
It's quite difficult to get louder and softer on the Piano.
Think of the arm and wrist helping the fingers to get louder by adding some extra weight.

Using any notes in the ♮♮♮♮ make up some mood music that follows these Dynamics: $f > p < f$

Two suggestions:
1. a game of sport
2. a railway journey
(the Dynamics could change when the train goes into a tunnel!)

What Dynamics would you use for:

1. a Lullaby
2. a March
3. a piece about Eric meeting Bradley
4. a piece about an aeroplane?

actually — ! always write about the same thing..

Warm-up

Copy this Warm-up into your Manuscript Book

DYNAMIC ERIC

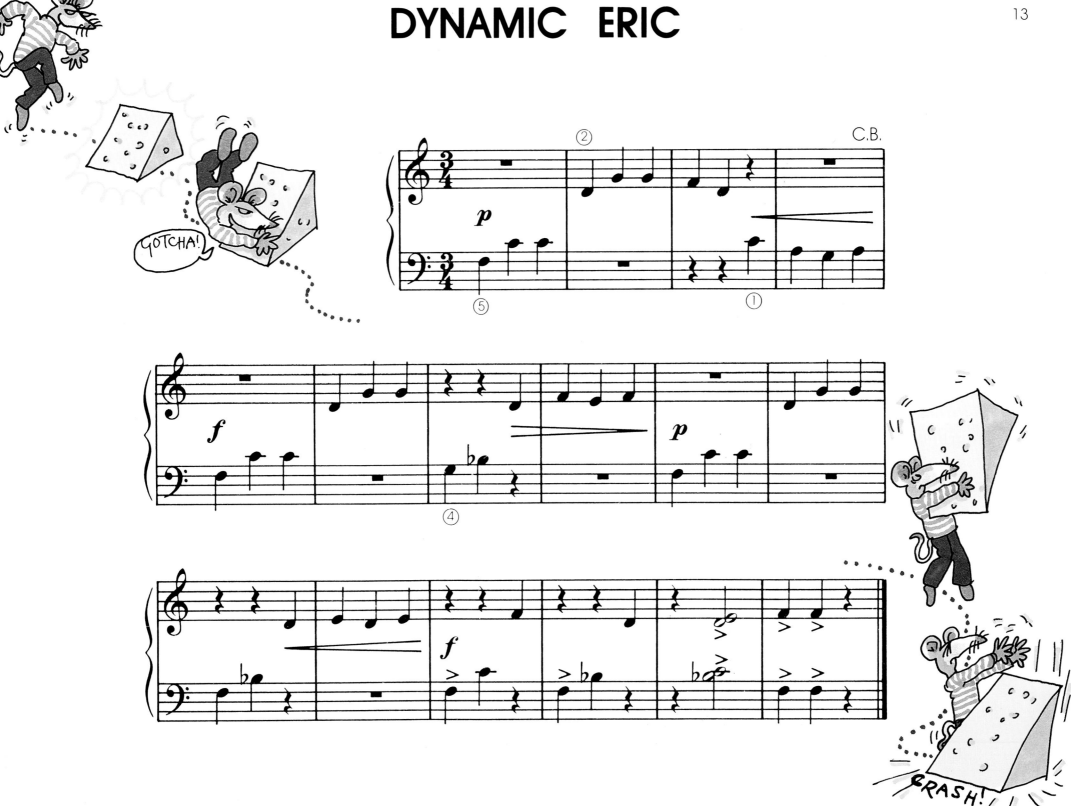

PHRASE—MARKS

A **Phrase-mark** is a long curved line over a musical sentence.

Imagine taking a breath at the end of each Phrase-mark, and lift your hand off briefly **without changing speed**.

Say these words slowly in strict time, as your teacher taps out ♩ beats. Take a short breath when you see // .

STEP ON A CRACK

To help you, the sign // has been added in this piece, so that you know where to lift your hand off.

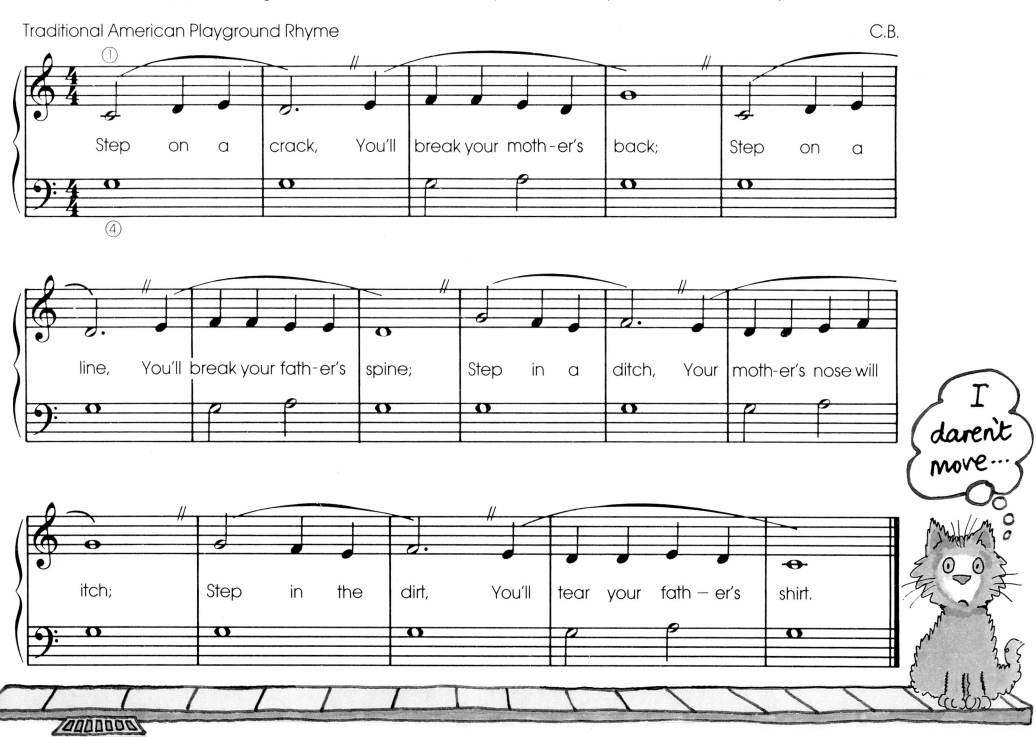

Traditional American Playground Rhyme

C.B.

F SHARP

♯ This is a Sharp sign

F SHARP is the black key just above **F**.

Until you reach page 33, the pieces will use **F♯** in the Right Hand only.

Remember, each ♯ sign lasts a Bar.

F♯   F♯

SHARPS GO TO THE RIGHT

SHARP♯

Think of Sharpen Up!

Play all the **F♯**s on the Piano. Use either hand, any finger.

Find all the **C♯**s and **G♯**s on the Piano.

Try playing **F♯** and **G♯** together as a Chord with fingers ② and ③ of your

Warm-up

Remember, always move your hand **towards** the black key.

SAINT PAUL'S STEEPLE

English Nursery Rhyme

f Up – on Paul's Stee-ple stands a tree, As full of ap–ples as may be; The

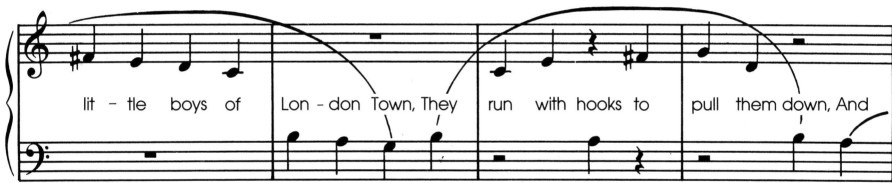

lit – tle boys of Lon–don Town, They run with hooks to pull them down, And

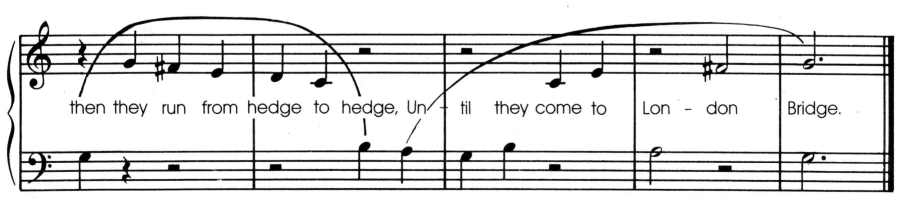

then they run from hedge to hedge, Un – til they come to Lon – don Bridge.

Supplementary material: Chester's Music Puzzles Set One, pàper 9. Warm Up With Chester Part One, p10. Chester's Piano Starters Volume One, p14.

sack for apples

TIME TO WRITE

Remember, use a B or 2B pencil.

1. Make all the **B**s flat.

2. Make all the **F**s sharp.

3. Use either a 𝅗𝅥 or a 𝅘𝅥 in each Bar to complete these Bars. Add the counts.

Count | 1 — 2 — 3 | 4 | 1 — 2 | | | | | |

4. Listen as your teacher plays this piece below. Add two Phrase-marks, some Dynamics and a Repeat Sign. Make up two sentences (of words!) to fit each Phrase.

HEAD ROCK

Do the movements below as two ♩s!

In Bar 4 nod your head twice
In Bar 8 lift your eyebrows twice
In Bar 12 wrinkle your nose twice

I'll give him head rock...

QUAVERS

A **Quaver** ♪ (or ♪) has ½ count. ♩ = ♪ + ♪

1 = ½ + ½

Two Quavers usually join together to make **1** count ♩ = ♫

Teacher says → walk   walk   walk   walk

as the pupil says → run-ning run-ning run-ning run-ning

Count the Quavers like this:

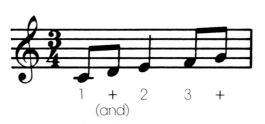

1 + 2 3 +
(and)

In your Manuscript Book write 4 Bars of ♪s in 2/4, using any notes between 𝄞 **C** and **G**.

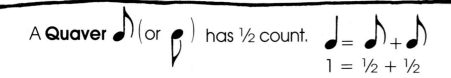

Clap these rhythms as you count out loud.

2/4

Count 1   2 +   1 + 2 +   1   2

and

3/4

1   2   3 +   1 + 2   3 +   1 – 2 – 3

"Parrot in the straw" sounds better...

Tap this rhythm on your right knee. It is the rhythm of **Turkey in the Straw**.

4/4

Count 4 + 1 2 + 3 4 + 1 2 + 3 4 + 1 2 3 + 4 + 1 2 3

TURKEY IN THE STRAW

American Traditional

GREEN GRAVEL

English Folk Song

Supplementary material: Chester's Music Puzzles Set One, paper 10.

TWO THEMES BY BRAHMS

Adapted from Johannes Brahms (1833 – 1897)
1. From Symphony No.1
2. From a Piano Intermezzo

ERIC ON THE RUN

23

DOUBLE-ACT

Second Player

Play the music on this page an Octave **lower** than it is written.

DOUBLE-ACT

First Player

Play the music on this page an Octave **higher** than it is written.

Supplementary material: Chester's Music Puzzles Set Two, paper 1.

KEY SIGNATURES

A **Key Signature** is written after the Clef to show which ♯s and ♭s are needed in the piece.

Scales and the names of all the different Key Signatures are looked at in later books, but try to remember **F Major** and **G Major**.

Look out for a Key Signature before you play, then look for the notes which are changed by this Key Signature.

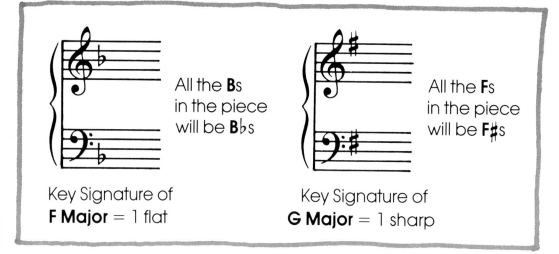

All the **B**s in the piece will be **B♭**s

Key Signature of **F Major** = 1 flat

All the **F**s in the piece will be **F♯**s

Key Signature of **G Major** = 1 sharp

like this...

Before playing the **Warm-ups** below, circle all the notes that are changed by the Key Signature.

Warm-ups

(G Major)

(F Major)

LIZZIE'S SNOOZE-TUNE

Accompaniment

What is the name of the Key Signature?

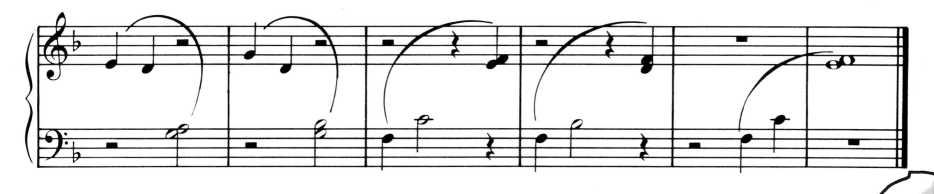

Supplementary material: Chester's Piano Starters Volume One, pp15 & 16. Warm Up With Chester Part One, p11.

MUSIC DICTIONARY
ITALIAN TERMS

Here are some Italian words to remember. You will often find them at the beginning of a piece of music to tell you how to play it.
(Look at Chester's Little Green Book for lots more Italian Terms.)

Andante = Fairly Slow

Largo = Very Slow

Adagio = Slow

Presto = Very Fast

Moderato = Moderate Speed

Allegro = Fast

Look through some of your teacher's music to see if you can spot any Italian Terms.

Which words would you use at the beginning of:
1. a Funeral March
2. a piece about a swimming race
3. a Lullaby
4. a piece about walking?

Add Italian Terms at the beginning of the pieces on pages 9, 13, 23 and 27.

ACROBATS

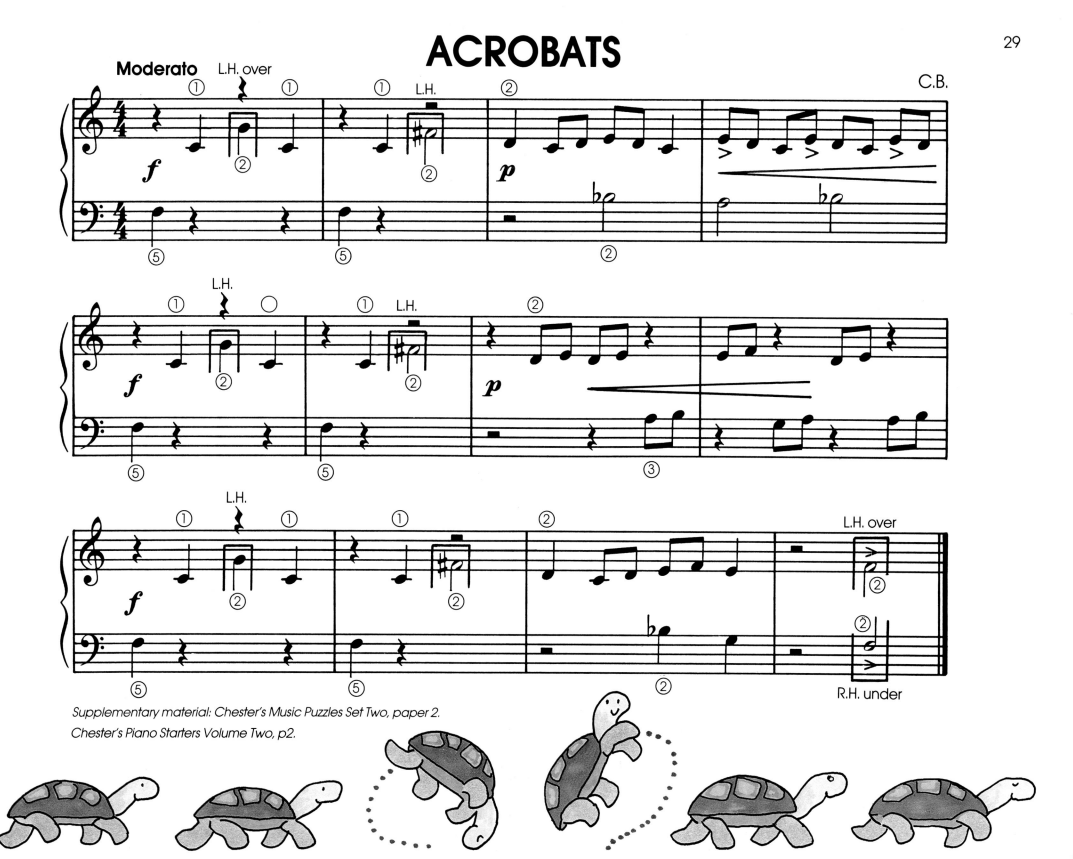

Supplementary material: Chester's Music Puzzles Set Two, paper 2.

Chester's Piano Starters Volume Two, p2.

The Left Hand plays **C** to **G**.

C D E F G

Find the C an Octave below **Middle C**, and put ⑤ of your Left Hand on it. This gives you three new notes.

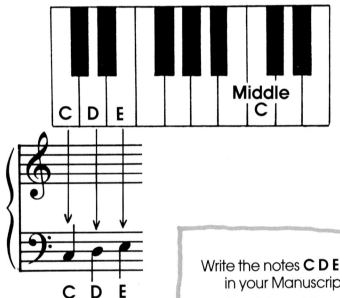

Middle C

C D E

Write the notes **C D E F G** as ♩s in your Manuscript Book.
Don't forget the 𝄢 sign.

Warm-up

Say the letter-names as you play.

NEW POSITION

STEMS

Look at the Stems.

Notes above the third line → Stems go down

Notes below the third line → Stems go up

Notes on the third line → Stems go up *or* down

3rd line

Write a tune in your Manuscript Book using the notes **C D E F G** in the 𝄢; 8 Bars in $\frac{4}{4}$ time. Start and end on **C**. Clap each 4-Bar Phrase first. Maybe you could add some words?

Mo will now demonstrate Stems...

WHEN THE SAINTS

*Try making a noise like a drum as you play!

Traditional American

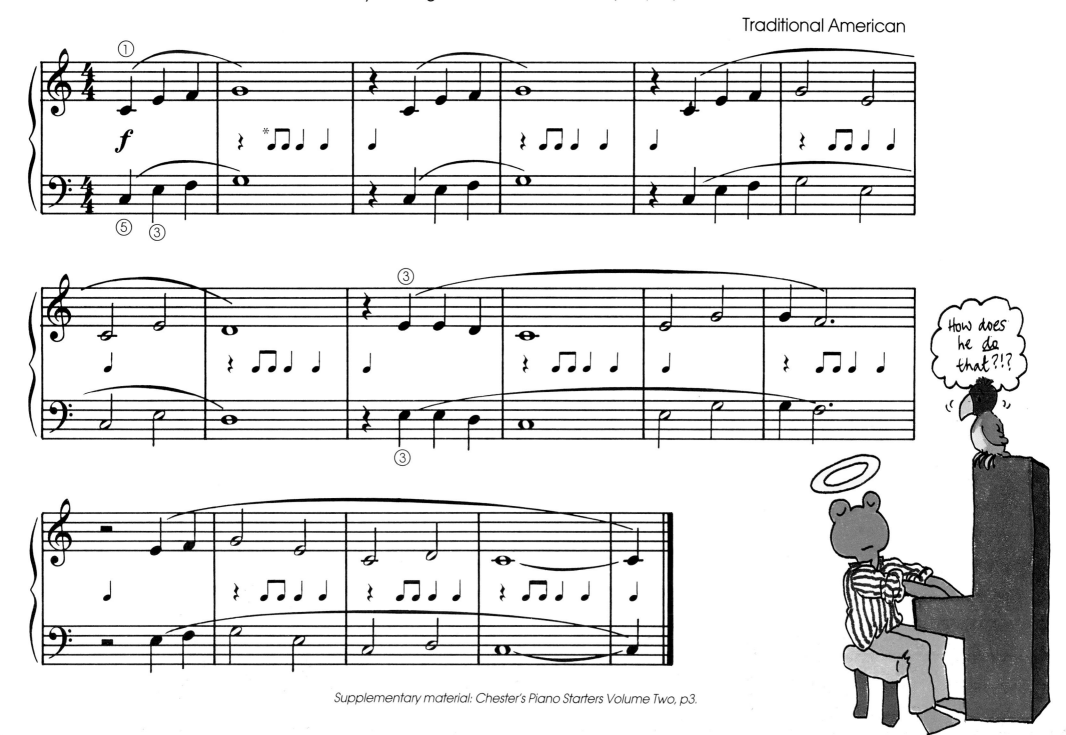

Supplementary material: Chester's Piano Starters Volume Two, p3.

THE CHASE

An **Octave** = 8 notes.
It is the distance from one note to the next note with the same letter-name.
Can you spot where the hands are playing an Octave apart in the piece below?

C to C.

Adapted from Nicolai Paganini (1782−1840)

JUNIOR'S WHISTLING SONG

D.C. (Da Capo) = Go back to the beginning and play until you see the word **Fine**

Fine = The End.   Try whistling the first two Phrases as you play!

French Folk Song

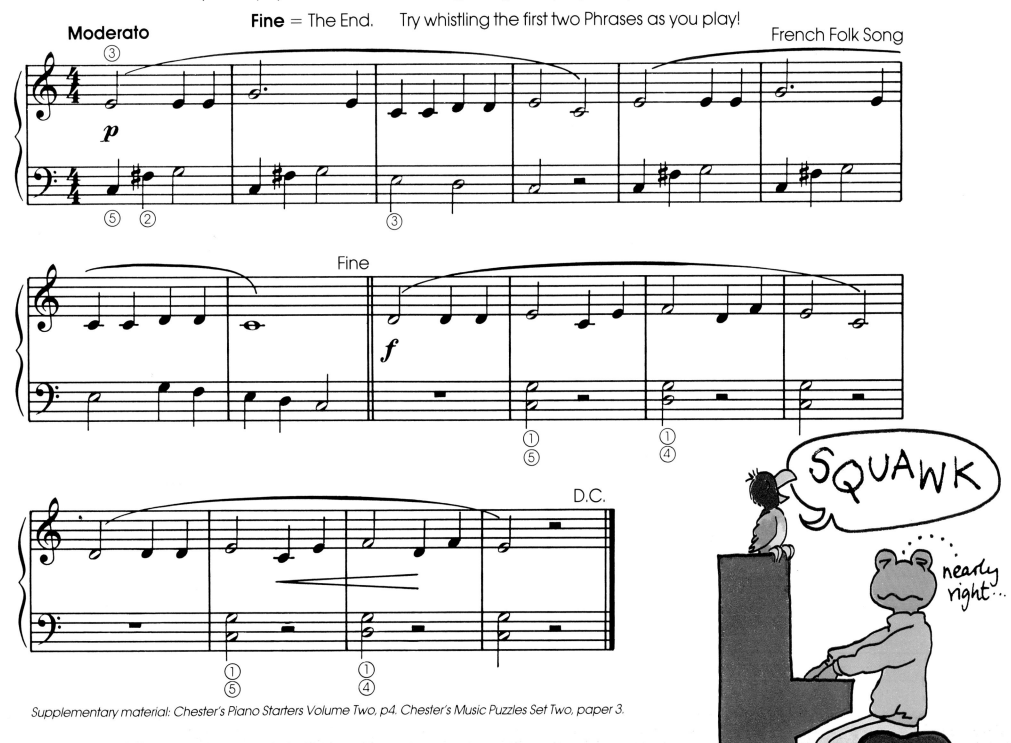

Supplementary material: Chester's Piano Starters Volume Two, p4. Chester's Music Puzzles Set Two, paper 3.

ANOTHER FLAT — E♭

E♭   E♭

Look at these new notes above.

Remember: Flats go to the left.   Flatten Down!

Play all the **E♭**s on the Piano.
Use either hand, any finger.

Now play the two **E♭**s at the
top of this page
with finger ③ for the 𝄞
and finger ③ for the 𝄢

In your Manuscript Book write:
1. 4 𝄞 **E♭**s in one bar of 𝟑/𝟒
2. 4 𝄢 **E♭**s in one bar of 𝟐/𝟒

Warm-ups

NORTHERN SONG

Supplementary material: Warm Up With Chester Part One, pp12 & 13. Chester's Piano Starters Volume Two, p5.

THE MAN WHO WASN'T THERE

Make sure you play this piece **Legato**

Words Anon.

C.B.

SCHOOLDAYS!

C.B.

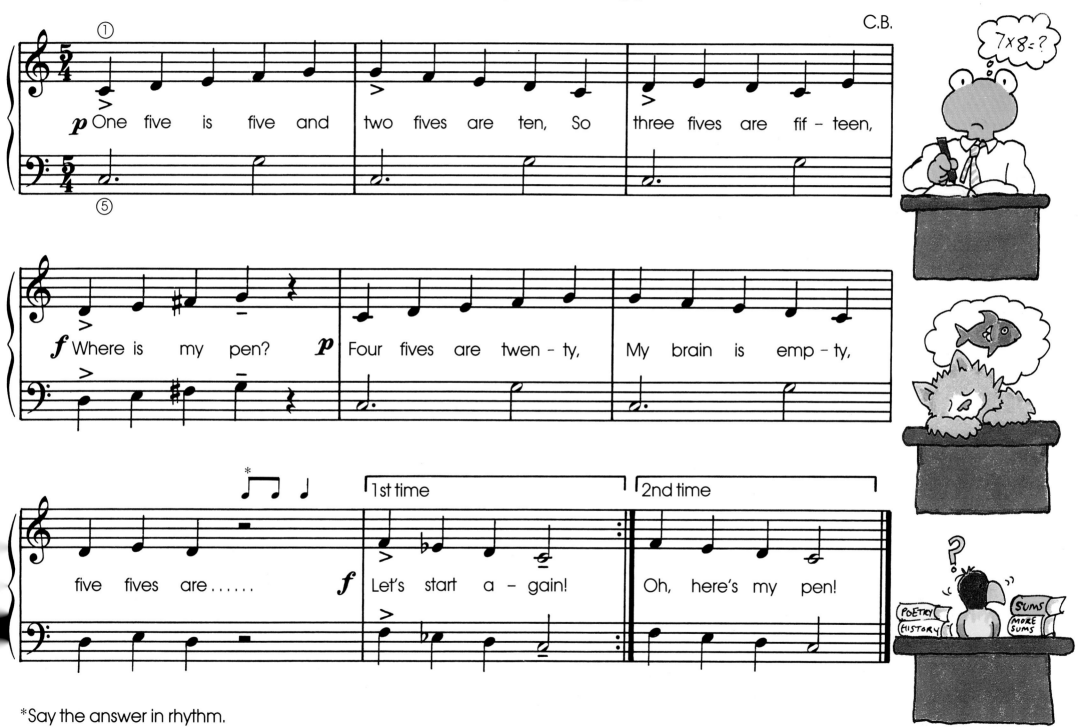

*Say the answer in rhythm.

MIDDLE D

New position: Left Hand plays **D** to **G**

D   C   B   A   G

Find the **D** a Step above **Middle C**
and put ① of your Left Hand on it.
Your Left Hand is now playing **D** to **G**.

Middle D can be
written in either Clef.

Both these notes are the **D**
a Step above **Middle C**.

ANOTHER SHARP — C♯

Remember: Sharps go to the right.
Sharpen Up!

Write these notes
Middle D, C, B, A, G, as ♩s
in your Manuscript Book.
Don't forget the 𝄢 sign!

With fingers ① and ② of your
practise playing **Middle D** to **Middle C**
to the rhythm of
Turkey in the Straw.

Play all the **C♯**s on
the Piano. Use either
hand, any finger.

Play this C♯ with
finger ② of your

there's a
lot to do on
this page

and
even
more o
the
ne

CRAYONS

Warm-up

TURKEY IN THE STRAW

What is the name of the Key Signature?

American Traditional

FORGET-ME-NOT

Louis Köhler (1820 – 1886)

Supplementary material: Warm Up With Chester Part One, p14.

RING—A—RING O' ROSES

Nursery Rhyme

*Cover some notes with your Right forearm and play them as a Chord!

MARCH FOR MO

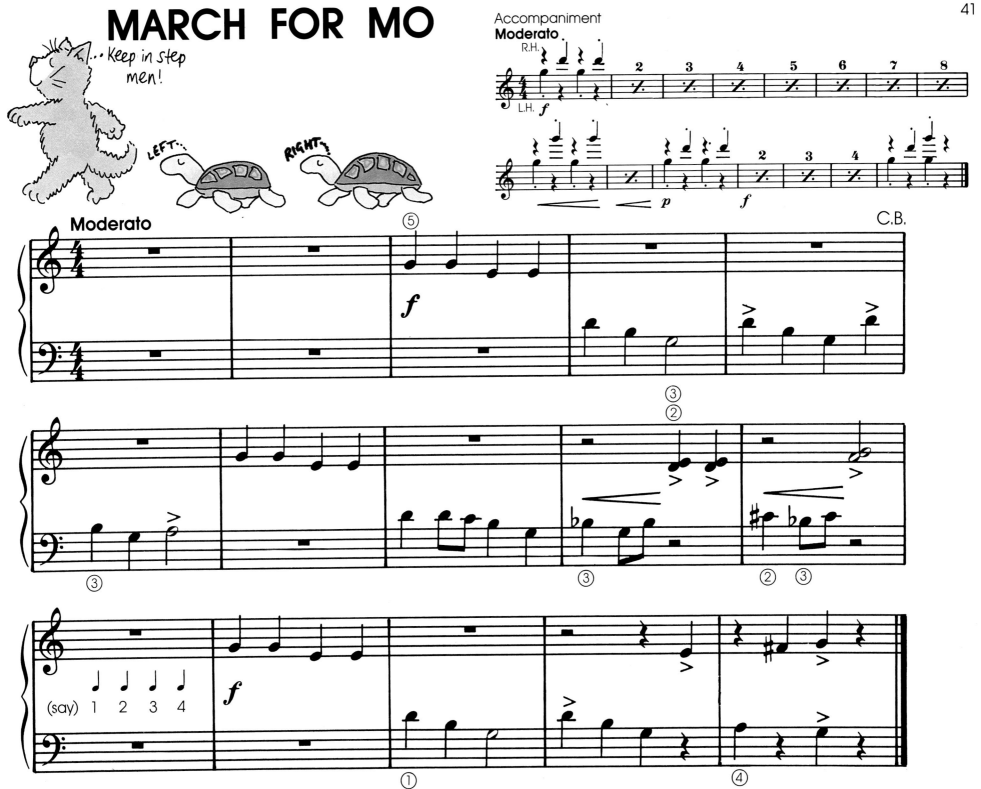

...keep in step men!

LEFT... RIGHT...

Accompaniment
Moderato

C.B.

Moderato

(say) 1 2 3 4

New position: Right Hand plays **B** to **F**

B C D E F

Find **B** a step below **Middle C**
and put ① of your Right Hand on it.
Your Right Hand is now playing **B** to **F**.

Middle B can be
written in either Clef.

Both these notes are the **B**
a Step below **Middle C**.

Write these notes
Middle B, C, D, E, F, as ♩.s
in your Manuscript Book.
Don't forget the 𝄞 sign!

NATURAL SIGN

♮ This is a Natural sign. This cancels a ♯ or a ♭ sign.

Any sign (♯, ♭, or ♮) that is **not** in the Key Signature is called an **Accidental**.

Cancel the ♯s
and ♭s in these Bars
by adding ♮s.

Warm-up

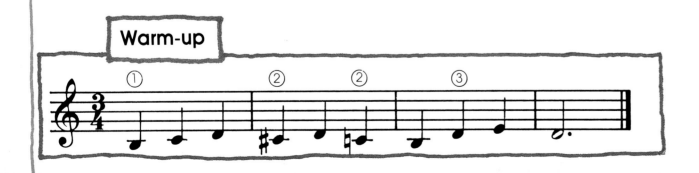

that wasn't an accidental, that was a wrong note..

ooops!

BRADLEY STAYS COOL!

Look carefully at the Key Signature and the Accidentals.

C.B.

Supplementary material: Chester's Piano Starters Volume Two, p6. Chester's Music Puzzles Set Two, paper 4. Warm Up With Chester Part One, p15.

NEW POSITION

New position: Right Hand plays **G** to **D**

Find the **G** a 5th above **Middle C** and put ① of your Right Hand on it. This gives you four new notes.

G A B C D

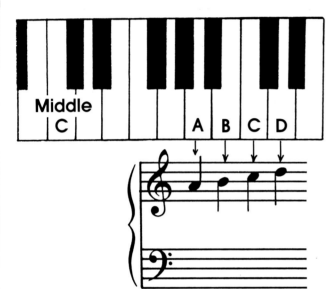

Your Right Hand is now playing **G** to **D**.

Write the notes **G, A, B, C, D,** as ♩s in your Manuscript Book. Look at page 30 for the rules about Stems.

page 30 is my favou...

Put your fingers on the notes of this new position, and play the following in any rhythm:
G G B B D D B B C C A A G D G

Warm-up

Say the letter-names of this Warm-up as you play.

We need a Warm-up..

GUESS THE TITLE

You should know it by now!

American Traditional

CRADLE SONG

Andante

Eduard Horak (1838–1892)

Supplementary material: Warm Up With Chester Part One, p16.

MAKING WHOOPEE

Watch out — the Time Signature keeps changing!

Supplementary material: Warm Up With Chester Part One, p17.

Chester's Music Puzzles Set Two, paper 5.

Well done, you are now ready for Book Three.

5/04 (5081C

Printed in Singapor

TRUE OR FALSE? Book 1 Answers:

TRUE OR FALSE?

Put ✓ for True and ✗ for False.

1. ♯ = a Flat sign.

2. Flats go to the right.

3. A Phrase-mark = a musical sentence.

4. 𝄢 = A 4th.

5. ♪♪♪ = 𝅗𝅥.

6. 𝄞 = Time Signature.

7. Legato = Fairly slow.

8. 𝄢 = Key Signature of **F** Major.

9. Fine = Go back to the beginning.

10. 𝄞 = **C**

11. Presto = Fast.

12. 𝄢 is the same note as 𝄞

13. Allegro = Fast.

14. D.C. (Da Capo) = The End.

15. 𝄢 = **B**

16. 𝄞 = **D**

17. ♮ = a Natural sign.

18. 𝄞 is the same note as 𝄢

19. 𝄞 = **E♭**

20. 𝄢 = **A**

The answers are in Book Three.

Certificate

This is to certify that ....

has successfully completed Book 2 of Chester's Easiest Piano Course,

and is promoted to Book 3.

CONGRATULATIONS

Signed (Teacher) ....

Date ....